THE BODY IN EQUIPOISE

poems

JOEL ALLEGRETTI

FCP

Full Court Press
Englewood Cliffs, New Jersey

First Edition

Published in the United States of America
by Full Court Press, 601 Palisade Avenue
Englewood Cliffs, NJ 07632
fullcourtpressnj.com

ISBN 978-1-938812-46-0

Book Design by Barry Sheinkopf
for Bookshapers (bookshapers.com)

Cover art, "Geometry," by Barry Sheinkopf

FCP Colophon by Liz Sedlack

"A work at once finely tuned, vast, and surprising, Joel Allegretti's *The Body in Equipoise* is, indeed, the 'human being squaring the circle,' with its 'nervous system. . .a radio tuned to the soundtrack of life.' Or perhaps this more accurately describes Allegretti himself, who in deft and subtle strokes has created a poetics from the bones and beams of centuries of architectural history (not to mention modern art) that is somehow both erudite and enduring, light and air filled—much like its inspiration. Further evidence of the highly original, remarkable work coming out of our small presses today."

—Lynne DeSilva-Johnson,
Managing Editor, *The Operating System*

"Joel Allegretti tells us, 'I am a creature of rooms.' Each of his stanzas is cantilevered above corridors of memory. The ghosts of Mies van der Rohe, Eero Saarinen, Antoni Gaudi, and Frank Gehry create 'dwelling[s] in the shape of the shapeless.' This architect of words voices selves, with linguistic sinew, with etymological marrow. The poet avers, 'Under the wing of a great architecture / Marble recovers its identity.' His personae chart peregrinations from the known to spires of the ineffable. With alacrity, the reader climbs each annealed line, arriving at a thrilling new language that is uniquely Allegretti's."

—Dean Kostos,
Author of *This Is Not a Skyscraper*
(Benjamin Saltman Poetry Award winner)
and *Rivering*

Also by Joel Allegretti

Europa/Nippon/New York: Poems/Not-Poems (2012)

Thrum (2010)

Father Silicon (2006)

The Plague Psalms (2000)

TABLE OF CONTENTS

"The body in equipoise, a phrase coined by the architect Sigfried Giedion, is a body that is aware of its surroundings and acts in them and is thus always collaging together itself and the world into a changing composition. The body in equipoise merges the body and the building into the active, and yet static, architecture of the self."

—Aaron Betsky,
"Bodybuildings: Toward a
Hybrid Order of Architecture"

Q & A

We saw you. Tell us.

1:15 a.m.
I stepped out my front door,
    descended the steps.
A thin shower whispered down;
    it and the heat conjured mist.
I turned right, rounded the corner. . .

Which corner?

Where the priest died.
    Every day someone leaves
a memorial rose; tonight, someone
    left an icon of a saint.

Which saint?

St. Sebastian. The Sodoma portrait:
    stoic, humble, feminine even.
What we expect of all our saints.
    I passed a store and paused
to look in the window.

Which store?

The bookshop that sells nothing
    except scientific texts.
The owner looks like Borges.

After that?

The drizzle lifted,
    but the fog still bound me.
A world of rain smoke.

I strolled by the theater.

Which theater?

They closed it ten years ago
after the balcony incidents.

They reopened it, no?

As a commercial space:
Medical lab.
Collection agency.
Daycare center.

Where did you go next?

The cemetery. To visit a grave.

Which grave?

With the blank headstone.
I saw a woman once.
Weeping for her father,
her hair tied in a French twist.
The grass had dyed her knees.
Her eyes were blue.

Which blue?

A blind man might imagine the sea.

Which sea?

Off the coast of Iceland,
where the Cod Wars with Britain
were waged.

Then?

I returned home at two o'clock,
    brewed a cup of Darjeeling,
sat down to write my poem.

Which poem?

This one.

MAIN STREET, 8:40 A.M.

. . .the fog is lifting.

THE BODY IN EQUIPOISE

conforms to the angles of a labyrinth. Tastes the reds and violets of music. Is practiced at B, beth, and beta. Is the binding agent between earth and sky. Its sinews are house. Its muscles: landscape. Its bones: fence. Its limbs: cantilevers. Its nervous system is a radio tuned to the soundtrack of life. It is "the human being squaring the circle."[1] It is the human being squaring "the human being squaring the circle." Is the art museum of the world. Is architecture itself.

[1]Aaron Betsky. "Bodybuildings: Toward a Hybrid Order of Architecture."

THE PALAZZO DELLA CANCELLERIA IN ROME RECONSIDERED AS A POEM UNTO ITSELF

Every room
is
a stanza.

DA VINCI'S JOSEPH CORNELL BOX

Many flowers drawn from nature
A head, full face, with curly hair
Certain figures of St. Jerome
Measurements of a figure
Drawings of furnaces
A head of the Duke
Many designs for knots
4 studies for the panel of St. Angelo
A small composition of Girolamo de Figline
A head of Christ made with the pen
8 St. Sebastians
Several compositions of angels
A chalcedony
A head in profile with fine hair
Some bodies seen in perspective
Some machines for ships
Some machines for waterworks
A portrait head of Attalante raising his face
The head of Jeronimo da Feglino
The head of Gian Francesco Boso
Many throats of old women
Several heads of old men
Several nude figures, complete
Several arms, legs, feet, and postures
A Madonna, finished
Another almost finished, in profile
A head of Our Lady ascending into heaven
A head of an old man with a very long neck
A head of a gypsy
A head with a hat on
A representation of the Passion, made in relief
A head of a girl with knotted braids
A head with a coiffure

MOSQUE

In English, the Muslim house of worship is known as "mosque," a word deriving not from the official language of Islam – Arabic – but from French, *mosquee*, and Italian, *moschea*. The faithful refer to it as *masjid*, which comes from *sajada*, Arabic drawing upon Arabic. *Sajada* means "to prostrate oneself." Compare this to the etymologies of the mosque's antecedents, "church" and "synagogue." The paternity of "church" is traced to the Greek *kyriakon*, which translates unambiguously as "Lord's house." "Synagogue" has a similarly Hellenistic pedigree: *synagoge*, or "assembly."

Prostration implies servility, an association that conforms to Islam's fundamental tenet, willing and utter subservience to the Almighty. *Islam* itself means "submission."[1]

To the uninitiated, the mosque's most prominent architectural constituents are the domed ceiling and the minarets. For the devout, the supreme feature is the *mihrab*, a niche in the wall that identifies the direction of Mecca, birthplace of the Prophet Muhammad (PBUH[2]). During prayer, offered at five prescribed times each day, Muslims everywhere kneel and bow toward this holiest of cities.

[1] In his biography of William S. Burroughs, Ted Morgan recounts a visit to the Tangier home of a Muslim friend by Burroughs' colleague, painter and artisan of the hashish brownie Brion Gysin. When the friend's father impolitely informed Gysin that prior to him, the only Christians who had ever been in the house were slaves, the worldly and diplomatic artist replied, "Are we all not the slaves of Allah?"

[2] Peace Be Upon Him, a phrase used by Muslims when referring to the Prophet.

AFTER GROPIUS

Under the wing of a great architecture
A green-tinted bottle is an article of the faith
And a parallelogram rises above itself.

Under the wing of a great architecture
Marble recovers its identity
And a painting recalls it is only a flat surface.

Under the wing of a great architecture
Piano tuners finally locate the key of π
And jazz opiates the social engineers.

Under the wing of a great architecture
Are[1]
And the need for more livable space.

Under the wing of a great architecture
Is the other wing.

---

[1]all the footnotes.

OUD AND OUD: A PRONOUNCEMENT

I doubt the great Dutch architect J.J.P. Oud, who between 1928 and 1930 designed the Keifhoek Housing Development in Rotterdam, ever played the oud, the Middle Eastern lute and queen instrument of Arabic music, whose subtle, yet rich, voice endeared it to many an emir. I think it unlikely, as well, that Oud was even familiar with the oud.

I, who do play the oud, would like to have played the oud in Oud's 1922 Garden Village in Rotterdam at Oud-Mathenesse, or perhaps the oud would have been more conducive to Oud's 1925 Café de Unie in Rotterdam.

I don't mean to be too loud about the accomplishments of Oud or unfairly subdued about the beauty of the oud.

FOUR RHAPSODIES (FOR MARCEL DUCHAMP)

I.
A urinal is
A specialized toilet

For urinating into
Generally used by males.

II.
In busy men's washrooms, urinals are installed
For efficiency: compared with urination in a general toilet,
Usage is faster because within the room there are

No additional doors,
No locks, and
No seat to turn up; also a urinal takes

Less space, is simpler, and consumes
Less water per flush than a toilet.

III.
A city famous for its street urinals is Paris, France.

IV.
Waterless urinals can save 40,000 gallons of water per year,
Based upon a typical commercial installation.
Further, this product has redefined the paradigm

For urinal design and functionality
By offering a virtually splash-free surface
Along with odorless, easy-to-maintain performance.

M.C. ESCHER

I am a creature of rooms
Blocks of space caged in walls
Corners tame them
Each one opens onto another. . .and another. . .
    and another
Escher designed ingress and egress
I give their floors a reason for being
Breathe their air
Clear my throat
I say, "I am Joel" [sotto voce]
To disrupt the quiet
My voice a water slider on a pond of silences

*

His family intended for Maurits Cornelis Escher (b. 1898) to pursue a career as an architect. Architecture was his father's profession. A career as an architect was tantamount to a family tradition. But his academic performance was unacceptable. His talent lay in drawing. An unacceptable academic performance and talent for drawing erased his family's ambitions for a family architectural tradition. With hopes for a family tradition neutered, the unacceptable academic performance and facility for drawing directed him to the discipline for which he is esteemed by mathematicians and commercial calendar publishers. M.C. the mathematical artist never destined for the architect's drafting table (d. 1972) is famous for "impossible structures."

*

My voice a water slider on a pond of silences
To disrupt the quiet
I say, "I am Joel" [sotto voce]
Clear my throat
Breathe their air
I give their floors a reason for being
Escher designed ingress and egress
Each one opens onto another. . .and another. . .
    and another
Corners tame them
Blocks of space caged in walls
I am a creature of rooms

THE EMPTY ROOM RECONSIDERED AS THE INTERIOR OF A PIANO

Step 1

Think of an empty room. Think of the echo in an empty room. Think of the echo in an empty room as a constituent part of an empty room, like the walls, ceiling, and floor. Think of an empty room as the resonant hollow of an acoustic musical instrument. Specifically, think of an empty room as the inside of a piano, formally called the belly.

Step 2

Choose a room in your home that can be converted with ease into an empty room. Put the furniture in storage or donate it to charity. Relocate the contents of the closet to other rooms.

Step 3

Install, one-third of the way down from the ceiling, a bridge[1] on each of three walls (skip the wall with the windows). The bridges must span the length of the walls.

Step 4

Buy piano strings. The standard medium-size piano has 230 strings.

[1]A wooden piece that lifts the strings of a musical instrument and, as a result, enables them to resonate.

Step 5

Purchase 460 bolts. Screw two rows into each of the three walls, one row along the top (two inches below the ceiling) and the other along the bottom (two inches above the floor). Apportion the bolts per wall as follows: 152, 152, 156. The top and bottom bolts will serve as 230 pairs and, therefore, must align.

Step 6

Fasten a string to each set of bolts. Make sure it is taut. The strings of a medium-size piano have an aggregate tension of 18 tons. You will not achieve this degree of tension. Nor will you be able to tune your strings.

Step 7

When all the strings are in place, toss objects at them. Spoons. Keys. Tupperware®. Run the blade of a kitchen knife along them as you would a stick along a picket fence. Open the windows. Gift the neighbors with your original, atonal, and out-of-tune music.

Step 8

If someone ever asks if you play an instrument, say something like "Yes, I play the guest room."

MAN RAY

> Cut out the eye from a photograph of one who has been loved but is seen no more. Attach the eye to the pendulum of a metronome and regulate the weight to suit the tempo desired. Keep going to the limit of endurance. With a hammer well-aimed, try to destroy the whole at a single blow.
>
> —Man Ray,
> Instructions for *Object to Be Destroyed*, 1932

Em*MAN*uel *RA*dnitsk*Y* lived and worked from 1912–15 in an artist's colony in Ridgefield, a 2.6 square-mile borough in northern New Jersey. To the northeast lies Fort Lee, a pre-Hollywood Hollywood and a superb vista for viewing Harlem from the Hudson River's other bank. Moonachie is northwest.

Studio Road and Art Lane are by virtue of their names Ridgefield's passive tribute to its Dada credentials.

Inventory of objects at the intersection of Studio Road and Art Lane:

A two-family home
A four-family home
A single-family dwelling
A stone house w/ red gable, red door, white fence
A street sign, red border, red block letters:
No Parking, Tues., 9 a.m. – 3 p.m.
A stop sign, red
A second stop sign, red
A fire hydrant, red, compassed by decorative rocks
and an American flag

A primary color is the order of the day here.

Note to self: Gift wrap boxes containing a metronome, a hammer, a photograph of the eye of a dead celebrity, and typed instructions. On Christmas Eve, leave one box in secret on the doorsteps at the intersection of Studio Road and Art Lane. To each box tape a card which has the following words in cursive handwriting:

Do Not Open
Till 11:55 p.m., New Year's Eve.
A Joyous Xmas Season to All.

THE AMPHISBAENA RECONSIDERED AS ARCHITECTURAL TEMPLATE

Blueberry Half Moon Lane East runs along the shore and parallels Blueberry Half Moon Lane West, which lies a hundred yards away contiguous to an abandoned service road. One house, only one, stands between the Blueberry Half Moon Lanes. It is a two-story gingerbread structure, an architect's simulacrum of a watercolor plate from a Victorian-era children's book.

*

A porch faces Blueberry Half Moon Lane East and regularly receives the spindrift's ablutions. To the right of the door through which you enter the house is a wooden plaque with a painting of a pineapple. The welcome mat is clean and proportional to the doorway. The porch is an especially strong vantage point from which to observe the sunrise. There is a rocking chair, circa 1970s, that serves this purpose well and embellishes the pacific experience. When you open the door and step inside, a beige foyer greets you. To your right are stairs leading to the upper floor. To your left is a forest-green parlor. The room's focal point is an upright piano, probably an antique or at least a family heirloom. A burgundy colonial chesterfield, lace doilies adorning its arms, and a set of upholstered high-back chairs, also burgundy, circumnavigate the instrument. Another rocking chair is at a remove, off in the corner by the window. Folded on the seat in a rectangle is a black-and-red checkerboard Afghan blanket, the kind sold at a community craft fair. The ambience here is that of a quaint bed and breakfast.

*

A porch faces Blueberry Half Moon Lane West and witnesses daily the dwindling glimmer of the setting sun. To the right of the door through which you enter the house is a wooden plaque with a painting of a pineapple. The welcome mat is clean and proportional to the doorway. The porch is an especially strong vantage point from which to observe the abandoned service road. There is a rocking chair, circa 1970s, that serves this purpose well and embellishes the desolate experience. When you open the door and step inside, a forest-green foyer greets you. To your right are stairs leading to the upper floor. To your left is a beige parlor. The room's focal point is an upright piano, probably an antique or at least a family heirloom. An indigo colonial chesterfield, lace doilies adorning its arms, and a set of upholstered high-back chairs, also indigo, circumnavigate the instrument. Another rocking chair is at a remove, off in the corner by the window. Folded on the seat in a rectangle is a white-and-yellow checkerboard Afghan blanket, the kind sold at a community craft fair. The ambience here is that of a quaint. . .

TOWARDS THE DESIGN AND CONSTRUCTION OF A HOUSE IN THE SHAPE OF WATER

Architecture in general is frozen music.
—Friedrich von Schelling (1775 – 1854)

O wizard of changes, water, water, water.
—Robin Williamson (1943 –)

Vitruvius doesn't address the subject in *The Ten Books on Architecture.* Neither does Le Corbusier in *Towards a New Architecture.* Neither does Rem Koolhaas in *S, M, L, XL.*

In *From Bauhaus to Our House,* Tom Wolfe considers buildings designed by Mies van der Rohe, Eero Saarinen, and Philip Johnson, but not this.

Architects have realized structures in the shapes of:

•a basket (headquarters of The Longaberger Company, a basket manufacturer in Newark, Ohio. Architect: unknown);

•a conch shell (private home on Isla Mujeres, Mexico. Architect: Octovio Ocampo);

•a teapot (gas station in Zillah, Washington. Architect: John Ainsworth).

None to date—not Garnier, not Gaudi, not Gehry—has brought into three dimensions a dwelling in the shape of the shapeless.

Career Counsel

Become that architect.

Step 1. Enroll in a distinguished school of architecture, such as California Polytechnic State University or Cooper Union, and earn a bachelor's degree.

Steps 2 and 3. To hold yourself out as an architect, you need a state license. Therefore, you additionally must:

- complete an internship with a firm;
- pass all seven divisions of the Architect Registration Examination®.

Think about an office by the ocean or at least a lake. For inspiration's sake.

Recognize that you'll have to fund the construction, since no one will commission it.

Know that your creation will attract notice and invite interpretation.

*

"Mediterranean," the Continental among us said.
"Red,"
held the Cairo-bred real estate
broker.
The architect, Chicago born and raised, shook his head.
"Lake Michigan."

FOR IMMEDIATE RELEASE

"HOUSE OF GOODBYE" OPENS AT MUSEUM OF ENTERIC REPRESENTATION

The Museum of Enteric Representation today announced the opening of "House of Goodbye," an installation by the theoretical artist and architect Nicholas **Σ**. The exhibition runs through 5 p.m. tomorrow, at which time **Σ** and a team of his students will destroy it in the presence of museum visitors.

The piece occupies the entire first floor and half of the second. The second-floor portion is closed to the public. The artist, however, has created "Goodbye Means Goodbye," a set of 501 23" x 29" multiples featuring black-and-white photographs of that section of the work. They are available on the second-floor landing at no charge.

Elaborating on the impetus for "House of Goodbye," **Σ** writes in an artist's statement, "Here is the room of the bed of final things. Where a lifetime's cookie jar of dreams and wishes is the last word of the last sentence of a paragraph. Science has advanced from background music to a concert program for a rapt audience. Religion is the coda, the diminishing strain as the bow decelerates across the violin strings. Silence, as John Cage knew, is itself a form of composition, notably when a lifetime's cookie jar of dreams and wishes is the last word of the last sentence of a paragraph that strives to describe the room of the bed of final things."

The Museum of Enteric Representation is planning a retrospective of **Σ**'s aerosol sculptures.

##

NOTES

Introductory epigraph and "The Body in Equipoise":

The quotes are from Aaron Betsky's essay in the catalogue *Fabrications*, published in conjunction with an exhibition of the same name organized and presented simultaneously by The Museum of Modern Art, New York; San Francisco Museum of Modern Art; and Wexler Center for the Arts, The Ohio State University, Columbus, 1998.

"Four Rhapsodies (For Marcel Duchamp)":

Parts I, II, and III are verbatim text from Wikipedia.
Part IV is verbatim text from a Kohler Co. product catalogue.

"Da Vinci's Joseph Cornell Box":

This is a found poem comprising a list of various studies and objects that Leonardo da Vinci took with him when he left Florence for Milan in 1482. The inventory appears in *Leonardo da Vinci* (New York: Reynal & Company, 1956).

ACKNOWLEDGMENTS

The author extends his gratitude to the following journals:

1110, "The Palazzo della Cancelleria in Rome Reconsidered as a Poem unto Itself"

The Associative Press, "The Amphisbaena Reconsidered as Architectural Template"

Exit Strata, "Towards the Design and Construction of a House in the Shape of Water"

First Literary Review – East, "Main Street, 8:40 A.M."

Fulcrum, "After Gropius"

Illuminations. "Oud and Oud: A Pronouncement"

Guide to Kulchur Creative Journal, "The Empty Room Reconsidered as the Interior of a Piano"

Maintenant: A Journal of Contemporary Dada Writing &Art, "Four Rhapsodies (For Marcel Duchamp)"

Moonshot, "For Immediate Release: 'House of Goodbye' Opens at Museum of Enteric Representation"

New Mexico Poetry Review, "Q & A"

Out of Our, "M.C. Escher"

Sentence: A Journal of Prose Poetics, "Man Ray"

Xcp: Cross-Cultural Poetics, "Mosque"

Whiskey Island, "Da Vinci's Joseph Cornell Box"

"The Body in Equipoise" appeared in a multiple from Marymark Press, East Windsor, N.J.

ABOUT THE AUTHOR

Joel Allegretti is the author of four previous collections of poetry. His second book, *Father Silicon* (The Poet's Press, 2006), was selected by *The Kansas City Star* as one of 100 Noteworthy Books of 2006.

He is the editor of *Rabbit Ears: TV Poems* (NYQ Books, 2015), the first anthology of poetry about the mass medium.

Allegretti has published his poems in *The New York Quarterly, Smartish Pace, PANK, Barrow Street,* and many other national journals, as well as in journals published in Canada, the United Kingdom, Belgium, and India.

His fiction has appeared in *The MacGuffin, The Adroit Journal,* and *The Nassau Review,* among other literary journals. His performance work and theater pieces have been staged at La MaMa Experimental Theater, Medicine Show Theater, the Cornelia Street Café, and Side-Walk Café, all in New York.

Allegretti wrote the texts for three song cycles by Frank Ezra Levy, whose work is released on Naxos American Classics. He is a member of ASCAP.

www.ingramcontent.com/pod-product-compliance
Lightning Source LLC
Chambersburg PA
CBHW070752050426
42449CB00010B/2435
* 9 7 8 1 9 3 8 8 1 2 4 6 0 *